PHONICS CONNECTIONS

The U.S. Flag

by Celia Benton

capstone classroom

This is our flag. It is red, white, and blue.

It stands for the U.S.A.—the United States of America.

Our flag has 50 white stars. There is one star for each of the 50 states. It also has 13 stripes. They stand for the first 13 states.

This is an American flag from the past. It has 13 red and white stripes but only 13 white stars. The stars also stand for America's first 13 states.

Look for the red, white, and blue U.S. flag. It waves on flagpoles. It is in classrooms. It is in homes.

It is on stamps. It is even on the moon!

Wave the U.S. flag on the Fourth of July! Stand up and cheer! Be glad that our land is free!